THE WORLD'S 60 BEST PASTA SAUCES... PERIOD.
VÉRONIQUE PARADIS

PHOTOGRAPHER: Antoine Sicotte
ART DIRECTOR: Antoine Sicotte
GRAPHIC DESIGNER: Laurie Auger
COVER DESIGNER: Laurie Auger
FOOD STYLIST: Véronique Paradis
ENGLISH TRANSLATOR: Lorien Jones
COPY EDITOR: Emily Raine, Patricia Boushel

PROJECT EDITOR: Antoine Ross Trempe

ISBN: 978-2-920943-49-0

©2012, CARDINAL PUBLISHERS / LES ÉDITIONS CARDINAL
All rights reserved.

Legal Deposit: 2012
Bibliothèque et Archives du Québec
Library and Archives Canada
ISBN : 978-2-920943-49-0

The publisher acknowledges the financial support of the Government of Canada through the Canada Book Fund (CBF) for its publishing activities and the support of the Government of Quebec through the tax credits for book publishing program (SODEC).

Originally published under the title *"Les 60 meilleures sauces pour pâtes du monde... Point final."*

PRINTED IN CANADA

THE WORLD'S 60 BEST

PASTA SAUCES

PERIOD.

THE WORLD'S 60 BEST

PASTA SAUCES

PERIOD.

ABOUT THIS BOOK

The 60 pasta sauces in this book are, in our opinion, the 60 best pasta sauces in the world. Our team of chefs, writers and gourmets explored everything the culinary world has to offer to create this collection of the world's 60 best pasta sauces.

We based our recipes on the following criteria:

QUALITY OF INGREDIENTS

ORIGINALITY

TASTE

APPEARANCE

SIMPLICITY

Are these our personal favorite pasta sauces? Of course! But rest assured, our team of passionate, dedicated gourmets put time and loving care into formulating and testing each recipe in order to provide you with the 60 best pasta sauces ever. In fact, our chef brought each freshly made sauce straight from the kitchen into the studio—no colorants, no sprays, no special effects added—and after each photo shoot, our creative team happily devoured the very dishes you see in these photos.

We hope you'll enjoy discovering these recipes and using this book as much as we enjoyed making it.

TABLE OF CONTENTS

INTRO

Every one of the 60 best recipes in this book features a flavor and cost legend (see pages 018 and 019) to guide your taste buds as well as your wallet in choosing the perfect dish. You will also find a glossary of culinary terms (page 029), handy cooking tips and tricks (page 025), and a list of must-have kitchen tools (page 023) that will help you create the world's BEST recipes. Finally, use the easy-to-follow Table of Contents (pages 010 and 011) and Ingredients Index (pages 176 to 181) to find everything you're looking for.

Impress guests with your food knowledge from our informative "Did you know?" sidebars, and take your meals to the next level thanks to our tasty tips and serving suggestions!

Bon appétit!

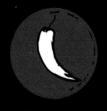

SPICY

RICH

TANGY

COST

LEGEND

HOT • PEPPERY • ZESTY

 LOW MEDIUM  HIGH

CREAMY • BUTTERY • LUSCIOUS

 LOW MEDIUM HIGH

ACIDIC • LEMONY • VINEGARY

 LOW MEDIUM HIGH

COST OF INGREDIENTS

 LOW MEDIUM HIGH

A SHORT HISTORY OF PASTA SAUCE

What is a sauce, exactly? A sauce is generally defined as a liquid, creamy, or semi-solid food that is poured over or prepared with another dish in order to add flavor and moisture.

It goes without saying that the history of pasta sauces is closely linked to the invention of pasta. Without pasta, there would be no pasta sauce! Although pasta has become a world famous hallmark of Italian cuisine, the first evidence of noodles can be traced back to ancient China, roughly 4,000 years ago. Pasta was actually introduced to Italy by Arabs during their conquest of Sicily in the 7th century. When Catherine de Medici married Henry II in 1533, she brought pasta to France and its popularity quickly spread across Europe.

Certain sauces have become celebrated across the globe thanks to the reputation of the chefs behind their creation, or simply because they're absolutely delicious. Alfredo sauce, for example, made originally with just butter and Parmesan cheese, was invented at the turn of the 20th century by an Italian restaurateur—named Alfredo, of course—to satisfy his pregnant wife's cravings.

When it comes to pasta sauce, what usually comes to mind is the traditional Italian tomato-based sauce. But the possibilities are truly endless! Try creating your own Asian-inspired sauces, cream sauces, or cheese sauces, or just add a drizzle of oil and a handful of fresh herbs to your favorite pasta. Let your imagination run wild!

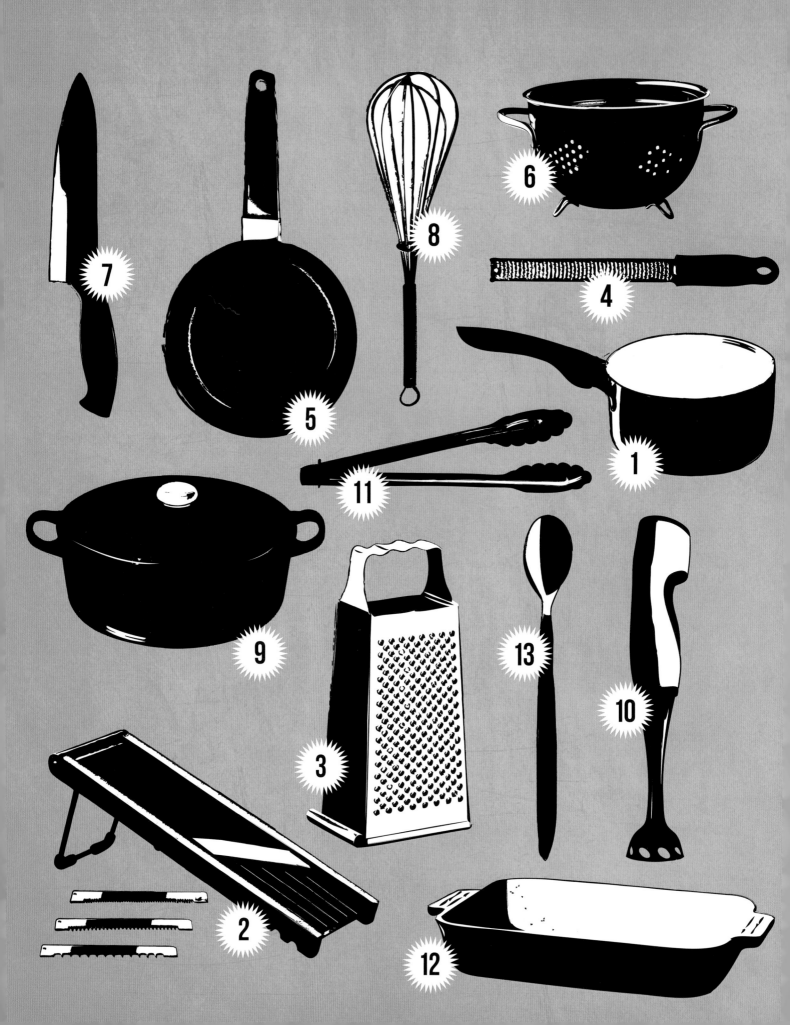

MUST-HAVE TOOLS

WHAT YOU NEED TO MAKE THE WORLD'S BEST PASTA SAUCES

1. A **small pot** for making sauces

2. A **mandoline** for perfectly sliced or julienned vegetables

3. A **cheese grater** for grating cheese

4. A **zester** or small grater for zesting citrus fruits

5. A **large frying pan** for cooking

6. A **colander** for draining pasta and any sauce ingredients that require draining

7. A **chef's knife** for chopping, cubing, dicing and mincing

8. A **whisk** for incorporating butter and making emulsions

9. A **Dutch oven** or heavy-bottomed oven-safe pot for slow-cook sauces

10. A **hand blender** for making pesto or easy mixing

11. A quality pair of **stainless steel tongs** for flipping meat, poultry and seafood

12. A **casserole dish** for making gratins

13. A **large spoon** for stirring sauces

TIPS & TRICKS

FOR CREATING THE WORLD'S BEST PASTA SAUCES

1. The key to making the best pasta sauces is using only the best ingredients.

2. One serving of long pasta is generally about a 1-inch diameter bunch of dried pasta, but there are no set portion rules! Make as much as you want, depending on your appetite.

3. During tomato season, gather together with friends and family to prepare and jar your own delicious, fresh homemade tomato sauce! If it's not tomato season, use canned tomatoes—they're inexpensive and do the job just as well.

4. If you're stuck with a lot of leftover sauce, freeze it in individual 1-cup portions that are perfect for packed lunches. Some dishes taste *even better* reheated.

5. Don't restrict yourself to pasta! Combine your favorite sauce with rice, couscous, bulgur, or quinoa. Yes, you're allowed.

6. Are you a *serious* cheese lover? If so, go ahead and add as much as you want you can't really go wrong. Hard cheeses keep well in the fridge and even the freezer, so stock up!

7. If your tomato sauce seems overly acidic, gradually sprinkle in some sugar to cut the acidity. Just make sure to taste!

8. A thick sauce will coat pasta perfectly. To make sure it's the right consistency, dip a spoon into your sauce. If the sauce coats the back of the spoon, it's ready. If it doesn't, continue reducing.

9. Try out different types of pasta to shake up any pasta dish!

10. The best pasta sauces are often the result of whatever's in the refrigerator combined with a bit of imagination. Don't forget to give your creation a mouthwatering name!

HOW-TO GUIDE

THE SECRET TO PERFECTLY COOKED PASTA

Use 2 teaspoons of salt for every 4 cups of water.

Don't add oil to the pasta cooking water—the oil will coat the pasta and your delicious sauce won't stick.

Fresh pasta cooks much faster than dry pasta.

Cooking time depends on the shape and thickness of the pasta. Check package directions for exact cooking times.

Never rinse pasta after cooking. Rinsing washes away the important surface starch that helps the sauce cling to the pasta.

If you're cooking your pasta ahead of time, cool it first by spreading the noodles over a baking sheet and placing it in the fridge. Hot pasta continues to cook even after draining, and this technique will prevent it from cooking unevenly and sticking together.

Add a few spoonfuls of the pasta's cooking water to pasta dishes with oil- or butter-based sauces—the starch in the water will bind and thicken the sauce naturally.

Another method is to drain the pasta halfway through cooking and then transfer it to a pan along with the sauce of your choice. Add a bit of pasta cooking water to prevent the sauce from over-reducing. The pasta will pull in the flavors of the sauce and cook to perfection.

GLOSSARY

1. SEASON

To improve the flavor of a dish by adding salt and pepper to taste.

2. BLANCH

To cook vegetables briefly in boiling salted water.

3. BRUNOISE

A basic knife cut in which food is cut into very small cubes, about 1/8 inch.

4. DICE

A basic knife cut in which food is cut into cubes.

5. DEGLAZE

To remove and dissolve caramelized bits of food at the bottom of a pan in order to make a jus or a sauce.

6. THINLY SLICE

To cut into thin, equal slices.

7. SAUTÉ

To cook, stirring, over high heat in a pan, Dutch oven, or heavy-bottomed pot.

8. CHOP

To cut into small pieces with a sharp instrument (knife or food processor).

9. REDUCE

To thicken a liquid by evaporation over heat.

10. JULIENNE

A basic knife cut in which food is cut into long thin strips. A mandoline is often used for this cut.

11. SEAR

To cook in fat (butter or oil) at a high temperature to obtain a golden or brown crust.

12. ZEST

To remove the zest (outer skin) of citrus fruits with a zester, grater, or peeling knife.

THE CHEF'S SECRET

Every seasoned chef will attest that the real secret to creating a successful dish is to *taste! taste! taste!* Taste before and after seasoning, add some heat or a squeeze of lemon juice if you think your dish needs a little kick, or go ahead and double the herbs or even the cheese! The most important thing is to follow your instincts and your senses. Listen for that telltale sizzle, inhale the tantalizing aromas, and CONSTANTLY taste your food so you can get to know your dish in all its stages.

There you have it—the simple secret to creating delicious, original dishes.

CLASSIC TOMATO SAUCE

SERVES 4

INGREDIENTS

8 fresh Italian tomatoes
2 tbsp olive oil
3 cloves garlic, chopped
1 tbsp sugar
Salt and freshly ground pepper

PREPARATION

To scald tomatoes: Cut out tomato stalks. With a small knife, make a small cut at the base of each tomato.

Fill a large pot with water and bring to a boil. Plunge tomatoes in boiling water a few at a time, about 10 seconds or until skin starts to split. Remove from boiling water and plunge immediately in ice water to stop cooking.

Remove skin from tomatoes with your hands. Chop into cubes or purée with a hand blender or in a food processor.

In a pot, cook garlic in oil over low heat (being careful not to burn garlic). Add tomatoes and sugar and season with salt and pepper. Simmer over low heat for 30 minutes.

Garnish as desired with fresh Parmesan, basil, parsley, oregano, mozzarella, or olive oil.

CHEF'S SUGGESTION

The pastas we use in our recipes are just suggestions. There are hundreds of different types of pasta, so go ahead and get creative!

TASTY TIP

For a spicier sauce, add crushed red pepper flakes along with the garlic.

BASIL PESTO

SERVES 4

INGREDIENTS

1/4 cup (60 ml) fresh Parmesan cheese
1/4 cup (60 ml) pine nuts, toasted
1 clove garlic
2 cups (500 ml) fresh basil
1/2 cup (125 ml) olive oil
Juice of 1/2 lemon
Salt and freshly ground pepper

PREPARATION

In a food processor, combine Parmesan, pine nuts, and garlic. Add basil, olive oil, and lemon juice. Season with salt and pepper and purée until smooth.

For a creamier pesto, add oil in a slow, steady stream.

If desired, add other fresh herbs to your pesto. Use parsley, oregano, rosemary, or any herbs of your choice. Try walnuts instead of pine nuts if you're on a budget—it's just as delicious!

Serve over *orecchiette*.

TASTY TIP

Throw tradition aside and try out different herbs like parsley, oregano, or rosemary in your pesto!

SALMON, ORANGE & BEURRE BLANC

SERVES 4

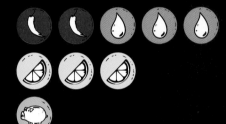

INGREDIENTS

1 tbsp butter
1 lb fresh salmon, cut into 1-inch cubes
2 shallots, minced
Zest and juice of 1 orange
1/2 tsp freshly ground pepper
1 cup (250 ml) cold butter, cubed
1 cup (250 ml) sorrel, roughly chopped
Salt

PREPARATION

In a large pan, heat butter and sear salmon for 2 minutes. Remove from pan. Sauté shallots, deglaze with orange juice, and add pepper and orange zest. Reduce until liquid has evaporated.

Remove from heat and gradually add butter 1 piece at a time, whisking constantly until sauce is smooth. If butter is no longer melting, put the pan back on the burner for a few seconds, remove from heat, and continue adding butter.

Stir in salmon and sorrel. Season with salt and pepper and serve over *linguini*.

 **DID YOU KNOW?**

Fresh sorrel actually tastes quite lemony. Try it for yourself!

EGGPLANT RICOTTA

SERVES 4

INGREDIENTS

2 tbsp olive oil
2 shallots, minced
2 cups (500 ml) eggplant, diced
1 tbsp rosemary, chopped
1/3 cup (80 ml) walnuts, roughly chopped
1/2 tsp paprika
Salt and freshly ground pepper
1 cup (250 ml) chicken stock
1 tbsp sherry vinegar
1/2 cup (125 ml) ricotta cheese
1/4 cup (60 ml) Parmesan cheese

PREPARATION

In a large pan, sauté shallots and eggplant in olive oil until golden brown. Add rosemary, walnuts and paprika and cook for 2 minutes. Season with salt and pepper.

Deglaze with chicken stock. Stir in vinegar, ricotta and Parmesan and serve over *farfalle* (bow-tie pasta).

DUCK WITH FOIE GRAS

SERVES 4

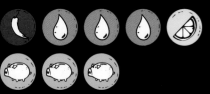

INGREDIENTS

2 confit duck legs
1 tbsp butter
1 shallot, minced
12 asparagus stalks, sliced diagonally
2 tbsp dried currants
1 tbsp brandy
1/2 cup (125 ml) chicken stock
1/4 cup (60 ml) 35% cream
1 tbsp canned foie gras
Salt and freshly ground pepper
1 tbsp sherry vinegar

PREPARATION

Remove meat from confit duck legs, shredding it into large pieces.

In a large pan, heat butter and sauté shallots, duck meat, asparagus, and currants. Deglaze with brandy and flambé. Add stock and cream and reduce until sauce is thick and velvety. Add foie gras. Remove from heat and stir until foie gras is fully incorporated. Season with salt and pepper. Add sherry vinegar at the end and serve over *papardelle*.

DID YOU KNOW?

Gavage, or fattening through forced feeding, goes at least as far back as Ancient Egypt, where carvings exist depicting workers grasping the necks of geese to enlarge their livers for foie gras.

SHRIMP & ZUCCHINI COCKTAIL

SERVES 4

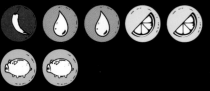

INGREDIENTS

1 tbsp olive oil
2 zucchinis, sliced
16 medium shrimp
2 cloves garlic, minced
Salt and freshly ground pepper
Zest and juice of 1 lemon
1 cup (250 ml) 35% cream
2 tbsp fresh Parmesan cheese, grated
2 cups (500 ml) arugula

PREPARATION

In a large pan, heat oil over high heat. Place zucchini slices and shrimp in the pan and let cook, undisturbed, until lightly golden. Add garlic and sauté. Season with salt and pepper. Add lemon juice and zest, cream, and Parmesan. Reduce until sauce is creamy. Add arugula at the end and serve over *ruote* or short pasta of your choice.

 **DID YOU KNOW?**

Zucchini can grow up to 3 feet long, but are usually picked when they reach about 8 inches.

THE CARBONARA

SERVES 4

INGREDIENTS

2 tbsp butter
2 cloves garlic, crushed
1 cup (250 ml) thick cut bacon, cut into small pieces
4 egg yolks
1 cup (250 ml) fresh Parmesan, grated
Salt and freshly ground pepper

PREPARATION

In a pan, heat butter and cook garlic and bacon. Remove garlic when it starts to brown.

Add cooked pasta (linguini or pasta of your choice) and 2 tbsp reserved pasta water. Stir.

Remove from heat and add egg yolks and 3/4 of the Parmesan cheese, and season with salt and pepper. Toss for 1 minute to thoroughly coat pasta. Garnish with remaining cheese and serve.

 **DID YOU KNOW?**

The original Italian recipe doesn't contain cream, but it is a common carbonara ingredient in other countries.

CHEESY HAM & LEEK GRATIN

SERVES 4

INGREDIENTS

2 tbsp butter
1 leek (white part only), brunoised
2 cups (500 ml) cooked, smoked or cured ham, cut into small cubes
6 leaves fresh sage, chopped
2 tbsp flour
1/2 cup (125 ml) white wine
1 1/2 cups (375 ml) milk
1/4 cup (60 ml) goat cheese
Salt and freshly ground pepper

PREPARATION

In a large pot, sauté leeks and ham in butter. Add sage and flour and cook, stirring, for 1 minute. Pour in white wine and keep stirring to prevent lumps from forming. Gradually pour in milk, whisking constantly. Simmer for 2 minutes, still whisking constantly. Add goat cheese and season with salt and pepper.

In a casserole dish, pour sauce over *cappelletti* or short pasta of your choice and broil in the oven until golden brown. Serve.

 **TASTY TIP**

Fry julienned leeks in a good amount of olive oil, drain, and sprinkle over pasta for a delightfully crispy garnish.

CREAMY CAULIFLOWER CURRY

SERVES 4

INGREDIENTS

1 tbsp butter
2 cups (500 ml) cauliflower, cut into small florets
2 shallots, minced
1 clove garlic, minced
2 anchovy fillets, chopped
1/2 cup (125 ml) water
1/3 cup (80 ml) cream cheese
1 tsp curry powder
1/4 cup (60 ml) toasted pine nuts
Juice of 1/2 lemon
Salt and freshly ground pepper

PREPARATION

In a large pan, fry cauliflower in butter until golden brown. Add shallots, garlic and anchovies and cook for 2 minutes. Add water and remaining ingredients, and stir until cheese is melted. Season with salt and pepper and serve over *farfalle* (bow-tie pasta).

DID YOU KNOW?

Cauliflower can also be green, yellow, orange, or purple!

OCEAN EXPRESS

SERVES 4

INGREDIENTS

1 tbsp butter
1/4 lb smoked salmon, roughly chopped
Juice of 1 lemon
3 tbsp brandy
1/2 cup (125 ml) 35% cream
2 tbsp capers, chopped
3 tbsp fresh dill, chopped
Freshly ground pepper

PREPARATION

Melt butter in a pan. Add smoked salmon, lemon juice, and brandy and cook for 2 minutes. Pour in cream and simmer over low heat for 5 minutes. Add capers, dill, and pepper. Serve over tortellini.

 **DID YOU KNOW?**

Smoked salmon is rich in Omega-3, a fatty acid that helps protect the cardiovascular system.

CRISPY FINES HERBES

SERVES 4

FOR BREAD CRUMB MIXTURE

2 tbsp olive oil
2 cups (500 ml) stale bread
4 sprigs fresh parsley
2 cloves garlic

FOR PASTA AND HERBS

1/4 cup (60 ml) olive oil
2 tbsp fresh parsley, chopped
2 tbsp fresh basil, chopped
2 tbsp fresh oregano, chopped
1 tbsp fresh thyme, chopped
1 tbsp fresh rosemary, chopped
2 tbsp fresh chives, chopped
Salt and freshly ground pepper

PREPARATION

In a food processor, pulse olive oil, bread, parsley and garlic until mixture is reduced into fine bread crumbs. In a large pan, toast bread crumb mixture, stirring constantly to prevent it from burning. Set aside.

Heat olive oil and add herbs and cooked pasta of your choice. Mix thoroughly. Season with salt and pepper, garnish with bread crumb mixture and serve.

DID YOU KNOW?

In the past, people sprinkled their pasta with bread crumbs when they couldn't afford cheese.

ARTICHOKE LOVERS

SERVES 4

INGREDIENTS

1 tbsp butter
2 shallots, minced
1 tbsp fresh rosemary, chopped
6 canned or jarred artichokes in water, drained,
rinsed and quartered
Juice of 1 lemon
1/2 cup (125 ml) water
1/2 cup (125 ml) 35% cream
1/2 cup (125 ml) fresh Parmesan, grated
Salt and freshly ground pepper

PREPARATION

In a pot, sauté shallots, rosemary and artichokes in butter. Add lemon juice and reduce for 1 minute. Add water, cream and Parmesan. Simmer for 10 minutes.

With a hand blender or in a food processor, purée sauce until smooth. Season with salt and pepper.

Serve over cannelloni or your choice of stuffed pasta.

 **DID YOU KNOW?**

When it comes to fresh artichokes, Americans are divided over their favorite dipping sauce— east coasters dip them in melted butter, while west coasters prefer mayonnaise or aioli.

CHICKEN GENOVESE

SERVES 4

INGREDIENTS

1/4 cup (60 ml) olive oil
8 fingerling potatoes, cooked and sliced into 1/4-inch rounds
2 chicken breasts, cut into cubes
1/4 cup (60 ml) white wine
1 1/2 cups (375 ml) green beans, cut in half
1/2 cup (125 ml) pesto (see recipe on page 034)
Salt and freshly ground pepper
Fresh Parmesan shavings for garnish

PREPARATION

Heat olive oil and sauté potatoes and chicken until golden brown, about 2 or 3 minutes. Deglaze with white wine. Add green beans and cook for 1 minute. Add pesto, cooked *farfalle* (bow-tie pasta) or short pasta of your choice, and 2 tbsp pasta water. Season with salt and pepper. Garnish with Parmesan shavings and serve.

PASTA CON LENTICCHIE

SERVES 4

INGREDIENTS

2 tbsp olive oil
1 onion, finely chopped
1 cup (250 ml) thick cut bacon, cubed
2 celery stalks, cubed
1 clove garlic, minced
1 tbsp tomato paste
1 cup (250 ml) canned brown lentils, rinsed
2 tomatoes, diced
1 cup (250 ml) beef stock
1/4 tsp cinnamon
2 cloves
1/4 cup fresh parsley, chopped
Salt and freshly ground pepper
1/4 cup (60 ml) fresh Parmesan, grated

PREPARATION

In a large pot, heat oil and sauté onions, bacon, and celery. Add garlic, tomato paste, lentils, and tomatoes and cook for 2 minutes. Add remaining ingredients and simmer over low heat for 10 minutes. Remove cloves and season with salt and pepper. Serve over rigatoni and garnish with Parmesan.

 DID YOU KNOW?

Cloves are the dried flower buds of the clove tree. They are extremely strong and aromatic and should be used sparingly.

SEASIDE SAUCE

SERVES 4

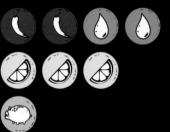

INGREDIENTS

1 tbsp olive oil
2 green onions, thinly sliced
1 clove garlic, minced
1/4 cup (60 ml) white wine
1/2 cup (125 ml) pitted black olives, sliced
1 cup (250 ml) canned diced tomatoes
2.2 lbs fresh mussels, cleaned
2 tbsp store-bought basil pesto (or see recipe on page 034)
2 tbsp fresh Parmesan cheese, grated
Salt and freshly ground pepper
1 tsp hot sauce (like sambal oelek)

PREPARATION

In a large pot, heat olive oil and sauté green onions and garlic. Add white wine, olives, diced tomatoes, and mussels. Stir, cover, and cook for 3 to 5 minutes, stirring occasionally.

When mussel shells are open, remove cover and add pesto, Parmesan cheese, and hot sauce. Season with salt and pepper and serve over *bucatini*.

BASQUE RED PEPPER SAUCE

SERVES 4

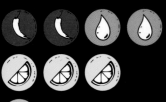

INGREDIENTS

2 tbsp olive oil
2 onions, thinly sliced
2 red peppers, cut into thin strips
2 yellow peppers, cut into thin strips
2 cloves garlic, sliced
3/4 cup (180 ml) white wine
Salt and freshly ground pepper
3/4 cup (180 ml) 35% cream
2 tbsp fresh marjoram, chopped
1/2 tsp piri-piri sauce

PREPARATION

In a large pot, heat oil and sauté onions, peppers and garlic until golden. Deglaze with white wine and season with salt and pepper. Cover and cook for 10 minutes over low heat. Reserve 1/3 of pepper and onion mixture, without liquid.

With a hand blender or in a food processor, purée remaining pepper and onion mixture until smooth. Transfer to a small pot and add cream, marjoram, and piri-piri sauce. Cook for 5 minutes. Serve over *buccatini* and garnish with reserved peppers and onions.

FETA, CREAM & WALNUTS

SERVES 4

INGREDIENTS

1 tbsp butter
1 onion, finely chopped
1/4 cup (60 ml) walnuts, toasted and chopped
1/4 cup (60 ml) white wine
1/2 cup (125 ml) feta cheese
1/2 cup (125 ml) water
1/4 cup (60 ml) 35% cream
Juice of 1/2 lemon
1/4 cup (60 ml) fresh dill, chopped
Freshly ground pepper

PREPARATION

In a pot, melt butter and sauté onions. Add walnuts, white wine, feta, water, cream, and lemon juice. Stir until feta is melted and sauce is creamy. Serve over spinach *tagliatelle* and garnish with a bit of fresh dill and freshly ground pepper.

MOROCCAN BRAISED LAMB SAUCE

SERVES 4

INGREDIENTS

2 tbsp vegetable oil
1 lb shoulder of lamb, cubed
1 medium onion, cut into large cubes
2 cloves garlic
1 sprig fresh thyme
1/2 tsp ground ginger
1 tsp cumin
1 tsp paprika
1 tsp ground coriander
1/2 tsp saffron
1/2 cup (125 ml) white wine
1 can (28 oz) diced tomatoes
1 cup (250 ml) small pitted black olives
Salt and freshly ground pepper
2 tbsp fresh basil, roughly chopped

PREPARATION

In a Dutch oven or heavy-bottomed oven-safe pot, heat oil over high heat and sear cubed lamb. Add onions and brown. Add garlic, thyme and spices and cook for 1 minute. Deglaze with white wine and add tomatoes and olives. Season with salt and pepper, cover, and cook in a 300°F (150°C) oven for 3 hours. Serve with short pasta of your choice and garnish with fresh basil.

DID YOU KNOW?

A Dutch oven is an oven-safe heavy-bottomed cooking pot with thick walls and a tight-fitting lid. It is typically made of cast iron.

TASTY TIP

Add dried apricots for a touch of sweetness.

JAVANESE CHICKEN

SERVES 4

INGREDIENTS

2 tbsp vegetable oil
1 chicken breast, cut into strips
2 green onions, thinly sliced
1 clove garlic, minced
1-inch piece ginger, minced
1 tbsp green curry paste
8 dried apricots, cut into 4
1 cup (250 ml) chicken stock
1/4 cup (60 ml) coconut milk
1 tbsp fish sauce
Juice of 1 lime
1/4 cup (60 ml) fresh cilantro, chopped
1/4 cup (60 ml) peanuts

PREPARATION

In a large pan, heat oil and sear chicken. Add onions and cook for 2 minutes. Add garlic, ginger, curry paste, and apricots and cook for another 2 minutes. Pour in chicken stock, coconut milk, fish sauce, and lime juice and reduce until sauce becomes creamy. Add cilantro and peanuts at the end and serve over orzo.

 **DID YOU KNOW?**

Peanuts are a part of the bean family and actually grow underground!

THE ARRABBIATA

SERVES 4

INGREDIENTS

1/4 cup (60 ml) olive oil
4 cloves garlic, crushed
1 tsp (or more, if desired) crushed red pepper flakes
or fresh or dried hot chilis, whole or chopped
1 small can (14 oz) crushed tomatoes
Salt and freshly ground pepper
1/4 cup (60 ml) fresh parsley, chopped

PREPARATION

In a pot, heat oil over low heat and add garlic and hot peppers of your choice. Cook for 10 to 15 minutes before removing garlic and chilis if they are whole. Add tomatoes and season with salt and pepper. Simmer for 8 to 10 minutes. Serve over spaghetti and top with parsley.

 **DID YOU KNOW?**

Arrabbiata, which means "angry" in Italian, is a red sauce with an extra-spicy kick.

THE CACCIATORE

SERVES 4

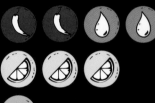

INGREDIENTS

2 tbsp olive oil
8 chicken drumsticks
1 onion, cubed
1 red pepper, cubed
2 cloves garlic, minced
3 sprigs fresh thyme
2 tbsp fresh oregano, chopped
1 tbsp sugar
1 cup (250 ml) white wine
2 cups (500 ml) canned diced tomatoes
1 tsp piri-piri sauce
Salt and freshly ground pepper

PREPARATION

In a Dutch oven or heavy-bottomed pot, heat oil over high heat and cook chicken until brown. Add onions, peppers, garlic, thyme, oregano, and sugar and continue to brown. Deglaze with white wine and stir. Add tomatoes and piri-piri sauce and season with salt and pepper.

Cover and cook in a 300°F (150°C) oven for 2 hours. Serve drumsticks whole or remove meat from bones. Spoon sauce over *conchiglie* (small shells).

 **DID YOU KNOW?**

Serve cacciatore over polenta to make this a truly authentic Italian dish!

22

THE VONGOLE

SERVES 4

INGREDIENTS

1/4 cup (60 ml) olive oil
2 cloves garlic, crushed
1/4 tsp crushed red pepper flakes
2 sprigs thyme
2 lbs fresh clams, scrubbed clean
3/4 cup (180 ml) white wine
12 cherry tomatoes, halved
Juice of 1 lemon
2 tbsp butter
1/4 cup (60 ml) parsley, chopped
Salt and freshly ground pepper

PREPARATION

In a large pot, cook garlic, red pepper flakes, and thyme in oil over low heat until garlic is golden brown. Remove garlic and add clams and white wine. Cover and cook, stirring occasionally, for about 10 minutes or until clamshells open up.

Remove clams from pot with a slotted spoon and set aside. Remove meat from shells if desired.

Add cherry tomatoes to the pot and reduce by half. Stir in lemon juice, butter, parsley, cooked spaghetti, and clams. Season with salt and pepper and serve.

DID YOU KNOW?

Spaghetti *alla vongole* is a traditional dish from Naples, Italy. Italians consume more clams than any other European country!

BLUE BLANQUETTE

SERVES 4

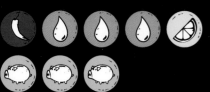

23

INGREDIENTS

2 tbsp vegetable oil
1 lb veal, cubed
1 onion, finely chopped
2 celery stalks, sliced
12 mushrooms, sliced
2 cloves garlic, minced
1 bay leaf
2 sprigs fresh thyme
2 cups (500 ml) chicken stock
Salt and freshly ground pepper
1/3 cup (80 ml) 35% cream
1/3 cup (80 ml) blue cheese, crumbled
2 tbsp fresh parsley, chopped

PREPARATION

In a Dutch oven or heavy-bottomed oven-safe pot, heat oil over high heat and sear cubed veal. Add onions and celery and cook until golden brown. Add mushrooms, garlic, bay leaf, and thyme.

Deglaze with chicken stock and season with salt and pepper. Cover and cook in a 350°F (175°C) oven for 3 hours.

When veal has finished cooking, remove from oven and discard thyme and bay leaf. Add cream, blue cheese, and parsley. Reduce over high heat until sauce is thick. Serve over long pasta of your choice.

For a less chunky sauce, shred veal with 2 forks before serving.

RAW SAUCE

SERVES 4

INGREDIENTS

4 Italian tomatoes
1/4 cup (60 ml) pine nuts, toasted
1/4 cup (60 ml) olive oil
5 large fresh basil leaves, roughly chopped
4 tbsp fresh Parmesan cheese, grated
Salt and freshly ground pepper

PREPARATION

Grate tomatoes, starting at tomato bases, into a bowl. Strain with a mesh strainer to remove excess juice. Put tomatoes back into bowl.

Add remaining ingredients to grated tomatoes. Season with salt and pepper and combine. Serve over stuffed pasta of your choice.

 **DID YOU KNOW?**

Raw foodism is the increasingly popular practice of eating only raw, unprocessed, organic foods.

THE STROGANOFF

SERVES 4

INGREDIENTS

2 tbsp olive oil
1 lb beef steak, sliced into strips
1 tsp mild paprika
1 onion, thinly sliced
12 button mushrooms, quartered
Salt and freshly ground pepper
1 clove garlic, minced
1/4 cup (60 ml) brandy
1 cup (250 ml) red wine
1/2 cup (125 ml) sour cream
2 tbsp fresh parsley, chopped

PREPARATION

In a large pan, heat oil over high heat and sear beef with paprika. Add onions and mushrooms. Season with salt and pepper and cook for 2 minutes. Add garlic and deglaze with brandy.

Flambé brandy and pour in red wine. Reduce liquid by half. Remove from heat and add sour cream and parsley. Mix well and serve over long egg noodles.

 **DID YOU KNOW?**

Beef stroganoff may have been named after the Stroganovs, a famous Russian family of successful merchants and landowners.

THE RATATOUILLE

SERVES 4

INGREDIENTS

6 tbsp olive oil
2 cups (500 ml) eggplant, cubed
1 red pepper, cubed
1 red onion, cubed
1 zucchini, cubed
2 cloves garlic, chopped
4 sprigs fresh thyme
1 bay leaf
2 fresh tomatoes, cubed
2 tbsp fresh parsley, chopped
Salt and freshly ground pepper

PREPARATION

In traditional ratatouille recipes, all ingredients are cooked separately, but using the same pan.

In a large pan:

Heat 2 tbsp olive oil and sauté eggplant. Transfer to a large bowl and set aside.

Heat 1 tbsp olive oil and sauté red pepper. Transfer to bowl.

Heat 1 tbsp olive oil and sauté onion. Transfer to bowl.

Heat 1 tbsp olive oil and sauté zucchini. Transfer to bowl.

Heat 1 tbsp olive oil and cook garlic, thyme, and bay leaf. Add vegetable mixture, tomatoes, and parsley and season with salt and pepper. Simmer for 6 to 8 minutes.

Serve immediately over gnocchi or serve cold.

DID YOU KNOW?

Ratatouille is a traditional French stewed vegetable dish usually accompanied by pasta, bread, or rice.

SAUSAGE, FENNEL & LEMON

SERVES 4

INGREDIENTS

2 mild or hot Italian sausages
2 tbsp olive oil
1 tsp fennel seeds, crushed
1 fennel bulb, thinly sliced
2 cloves garlic, minced
1/2 cup (125 ml) white wine
1/2 cup (125 ml) 35% cream
Zest and juice of 1/2 lemon
Salt and freshly ground pepper

PREPARATION

Cook sausages in boiling water for 5 minutes. Remove and slice into 1/2-inch rounds.

In a pan, heat oil and sear sausages until golden brown. Add fennel seeds and sliced fennel. Cook until golden and then stir in garlic.

Deglaze with white wine and cook for 1 minute. Add cream, lemon zest, and lemon juice. Season with salt and pepper and simmer until sauce is thick. Serve over spinach linguine.

 DID YOU KNOW?

The entire fennel plant is used in cooking: bulb, leaves, and seeds.

A TASTE OF PORTUGAL

SERVES 4

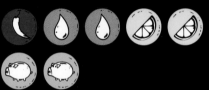

INGREDIENTS

1 tsp saffron
1/4 cup (60 ml) hot water
1 tbsp butter
3 slices bacon, cut into thin strips
1 onion, finely chopped
1 clove garlic, minced
4 canned boneless sardines
2 tbsp pine nuts, toasted
2 tbsp raisins
1 tsp sherry vinegar
1/2 cup (125 ml) 35% cream
2 tbsp fresh parsley, chopped
Salt and freshly ground pepper

PREPARATION

Infuse saffron in hot water for 15 minutes.

In a pan, cook bacon and onion in butter for 3 minutes. Add garlic, sardines, pine nuts, and raisins and cook for 2 minutes. Add saffron infusion, sherry vinegar, cream, and parsley and cook for another 2 minutes. Season with salt and pepper and serve over short pasta of your choice.

DID YOU KNOW?

Fresh, juicy grilled sardines are a summertime staple across Portugal! They are typically served with bread, potatoes, and a simple salad.

SAUCE ALLA GIGI

SERVES 4

INGREDIENTS

1 tbsp olive oil
1 onion, chopped
12 button mushrooms, quartered
8 slices prosciutto, cut into strips
1/4 cup (60 ml) brandy
1 cup (250 ml) canned crushed tomatoes
1/2 cup (125 ml) 35% cream
Salt and freshly ground pepper

PREPARATION

In a large pan, sauté onions in olive oil. Add mushrooms and prosciutto and cook for 3 minutes. Deglaze with brandy and simmer for 1 minute. Add tomatoes, cream, salt and pepper and reduce until sauce is rich and creamy. Serve over tortellini and top with a generous helping of grated Parmesan cheese.

BEEF & MUSHROOM RAGOUT

SERVES 4

INGREDIENTS

1/4 cup (60 ml) vegetable oil
2 1/4 lbs beef stew meat, cubed
2 onions, chopped
2 sprigs fresh rosemary
24 small button mushrooms
1 can (6 oz) tomato paste
1 cup (250 ml) white wine
2 cups (500 ml) beef stock
2 tomatoes, diced
Salt and freshly ground pepper
1/3 cup (80 ml) 35% cream (optional)
1/3 cup (80 ml) fresh parsley, chopped

PREPARATION

In a Dutch oven or heavy-bottomed oven-safe pot, heat oil over high heat and sear beef. Add onion, rosemary, mushrooms, and tomato paste and cook for 2 minutes. Deglaze with white wine. Add beef stock and tomatoes and season with salt and pepper. Cover and cook in a 350°F (175°C) oven for 3 hours.

Remove from oven and add cream and parsley. Place pot back on the stovetop and reduce until sauce is thick. Shred beef and serve over *conchiglie* (shells).

AUTUMN DELIGHT

SERVES 4

FOR ROASTED SQUASH

2 cups (500 ml) butternut squash, peeled, seeded and cut into 1-inch cubes
3 sprigs fresh thyme
2 tbsp olive oil
Salt and freshly ground pepper

FOR SAUCE

1 tbsp butter
2 shallots, minced
4 slices prosciutto, cut into strips
1/4 cup (60 ml) white wine
6 leaves fresh sage, chopped
3/4 cup (180 ml) chicken stock
Zest of 1/2 lemon
1/4 cup (60 ml) 35% cream
Salt and freshly ground pepper

Pumpkin seeds for garnish

PREPARATION

For roasted squash: In a bowl, mix together cubed squash, thyme, oil, salt and pepper. Spread evenly on a baking sheet and cook in a 400°F (200°C) oven for 30 minutes.

In a large pot, heat butter and sauté shallots and prosciutto. Add roasted squash, white wine, sage, chicken stock, lemon zest, and cream. Lightly mash squash with a fork. Reduce for 3 to 4 minutes or until sauce becomes thick.

Serve over spaghetti and garnish with pumpkin seeds.

 **TASTY TIP**

If you're crazy for cheese, add a few dollops of goat cheese or mascarpone to this recipe!

SPAGHETTI & MEATBALLS

SERVES 4

FOR MEATBALLS

1 cup (250 ml) bread, cut into cubes
1/2 cup (125 ml) 15% cream
1 tbsp fresh thyme, chopped
1 sprig fresh rosemary, leaves only
1/4 cup fresh Parmesan cheese, grated
1/2 lb ground beef
1/2 lb ground pork
1 egg
Salt and freshly ground pepper

FOR SAUCE

1 tbsp olive oil
1 onion, chopped
1/2 cup (125 ml) red wine
4 cups pomodoro sauce (see recipe on page 032)

PREPARATION

In a food processor, combine bread, cream, thyme, rosemary and Parmesan.

In a bowl, combine bread mixture, beef, pork, and egg. Season with salt and pepper.

Form into meatballs, about 1 1/2-inches in diameter. Refrigerate.

In a Dutch oven or heavy-bottomed pot, heat olive oil and sauté onion. Deglaze with red wine and add meatballs. Pour pomodoro sauce over meatballs. Cover and cook for 30 minutes over low heat.

Serve over spaghetti.

CHORIZO & ROASTED RED PEPPERS

SERVES 4

INGREDIENTS

2 red peppers
8 sundried tomatoes
1/4 cup (60 ml) water
1 tbsp olive oil
1 onion, finely chopped
1 cup (250 ml) chorizo sausage, sliced into rounds
2 cloves garlic, minced
Salt and freshly ground pepper
1/4 cup (60 ml) fresh parsley, chopped

PREPARATION

For roasted red peppers: Brush red peppers with olive oil and place on a baking sheet. Broil for 5 minutes on each side or until skin is charred and easy to remove. Cool in a covered bowl. Peel and seed cooled peppers, and then cut lengthwise into thin strips. Set aside.

In a food processor, purée roasted peppers, sundried tomatoes and water. Set aside.

In a pot, heat oil and sauté onions and chorizo for 2 minutes. Add garlic and stir. Add puréed peppers and tomatoes and season with salt and pepper. Simmer for 2 to 3 minutes. Add parsley and spoon over cheese ravioli.

TASTY TIP

To save time, use jarred roasted red peppers.

BROCCOLI BOUQUET

SERVES 4

INGREDIENTS

2 Italian sausages
1/2 broccoli, cut into large florets
2 tbsp olive oil
2 cloves garlic, minced
Salt and freshly ground pepper
1/3 cup (80 ml) white wine
1/2 cup (125 ml) water
1/3 cup (80 ml) 35% cream
Zest of 1/2 lemon
1 cup (250 ml) gruyère cheese, grated
2 tbsp cream cheese

PREPARATION

Remove sausage meat from casing.

In a large pan, cook sausage meat and broccoli in olive oil. Add garlic and cook for 2 to 3 minutes. Season with salt and pepper.

Add white wine, water, cream, and lemon zest and reduce for a few minutes. Stir in gruyère and cream cheese and serve over *fiocchi d'amore* or your choice of short pasta.

 **DID YOU KNOW?**

Broccoli is high in vitamin C, but its benefits are greatly reduced if it is boiled.

SCALLOPS, TOMATO & CILANTRO

SERVES 4

INGREDIENTS

1 tbsp olive oil
12 medium scallops, muscles removed
4 green onions, thinly sliced
2 cloves garlic, minced
1/3 cup (80 ml) white wine
4 tomatoes, diced
4 drops Tabasco sauce
Salt and freshly ground pepper
1/2 cup (125 ml) fresh cilantro, chopped

PREPARATION

In a non-stick pan, heat oil over high heat and sear scallops. Add green onions and garlic. Deglaze with white wine and add tomatoes and Tabasco sauce. Season with salt and pepper and reduce for 2 minutes. Stir in cilantro and serve over tricolor spaghetti.

 **TASTY TIP**

If you're on a budget, a less expensive flaky white fish, like red mullet, is an excellent alternative to scallops.

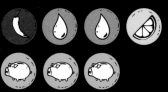

WOODLAND MOREL

SERVES 4

DID YOU KNOW?

Morels have a honeycomb-like cap and are highly prized by gourmet chefs for their nutty taste. Raw morels contain small amounts of toxins and should only be eaten fully cooked.

INGREDIENTS

1 tbsp butter
1 shallot, minced
12 medium morel mushrooms, cleaned and halved
1/2 cup (125 ml) walnuts, toasted and chopped
2 tbsp brandy
3/4 cup (180 ml) 35% cream
1/2 tsp nutmeg, grated
1 tsp sherry vinegar
Salt and freshly ground pepper

PREPARATION

In a large pan, melt butter and sauté shallot and morels. Add walnuts and brandy. Flambé cognac. Add cream, nutmeg, and sherry vinegar. Season with salt and pepper and reduce for 5 minutes or until sauce becomes thick and creamy. Serve over *pappardelle*.

GORGONZOLA DELUXE

SERVES 4

INGREDIENTS

1 tbsp butter
2 sprigs fresh thyme
8 slices prosciutto, cut into strips
1 cup (250 ml) chicken stock
1/2 cup (125 ml) 35% cream
1/2 cup (125 ml) blue cheese, crumbled
Salt and freshly ground pepper
2 cups (500 ml) baby spinach

PREPARATION

In a large pan, heat butter and sauté thyme and prosciutto. Add chicken stock, cream, and blue cheese. Season with salt and pepper and reduce until sauce is creamy. Add spinach 30 seconds before removing from heat. Serve over *ziti*.

 **DID YOU KNOW?**

Gorgonzola is a veined blue cheese made from unskimmed goat's or cow's milk, produced in Northern Italy and typically aged for three to four months.

GOURMET MUSHROOM & BACON

SERVES 4

INGREDIENTS

1 tbsp butter
2 onions, finely chopped
3/4 cup (180 ml) thick cut bacon, cubed
2 sprigs fresh thyme
2 portobello mushrooms, thinly sliced
1/2 cup (125 ml) red wine
1 cup (250 ml) store-bought demi-glace
1/2 cup (125 ml) old cheddar cheese
Salt and freshly ground pepper

PREPARATION

In a pan, heat butter and sauté onions, bacon, and thyme. Add mushrooms and cook for 2 minutes. Pour in red wine and reduce by half. Add demi-glace and old cheddar. Season with salt and pepper, stir, and cook for another 2 minutes. Serve over fusilli.

39

SUNNY PESTO

SERVES 4

FOR SUNDRIED TOMATO PESTO

6 sundried tomatoes in oil
Zest of 1/2 orange
2 tbsp water
1/4 cup (60 ml) pine nuts, toasted
1/3 cup (80 ml) old cheddar cheese, grated
1/3 cup (80 ml) olive oil
2 tbsp chives, chopped

FOR SHRIMP

1 tbsp olive oil
12 large shrimp, peeled
2 cloves garlic, minced
Salt and freshly ground pepper

PREPARATION

In a food processor, combine sundried tomatoes, orange zest, water, pine nuts, and cheddar cheese. Purée until smooth. Add olive oil in a slow, steady stream for a creamier pesto. Stir in chives at the end.

In a pan, heat olive oil and cook shrimp. Add garlic and cook for 2 to 3 minutes. Season with salt and pepper. Toss with pesto and serve over your choice of pasta.

 **DID YOU KNOW?**

Pesto is often confused with pistou. Pistou is a Provençal cold sauce, which, like pesto, is made with basil, garlic, and olive oil; the key difference is that pistou doesn't contain pine nuts or cheese.

RICOTTA PRIMAVERA

SERVES 4

INGREDIENTS

1/4 cup (60 ml) olive oil
2 cloves garlic, crushed
1/2 tsp crushed red pepper flakes
1/2 red onion, thinly sliced
1 carrot, julienned
1 yellow pepper, julienned
8 cherry tomatoes, quartered
12 snow peas, julienned
1 zucchini, julienned
2 tbsp fresh oregano, chopped
Salt and freshly ground pepper
1/2 cup (125 ml) ricotta cheese

PREPARATION

In a large pan, heat olive oil and sauté garlic and red pepper flakes for 5 minutes until cloves are golden brown. Remove and discard garlic. Raise heat to high and sauté onions, carrots, and peppers, about 3 minutes. Add remaining vegetables and cook for another 2 minutes.

Add *capellini* and oregano. Season with salt and pepper and stir to combine. Top with dollops of ricotta cheese and serve immediately.

OLIVIA SAUCE

SERVES 4

INGREDIENTS

3 tbsp olive oil
1 clove garlic, crushed
1/2 tsp crushed red pepper flakes
1/4 cup (60 ml) capers, rinsed and chopped
1/4 cup (60 ml) green olives, pitted and chopped
1/4 cup (60 ml) black olives, pitted and chopped
1 cup (250 ml) Italian tomatoes, cubed
2 tbsp fresh oregano, chopped
8 leaves fresh basil, thinly sliced
1/2 cup (125 ml) goat cheese
Freshly ground pepper

PREPARATION

In a pan, heat oil over low heat and cook garlic until lightly golden. Remove garlic. Add red pepper flakes, capers, and olives and cook for 2 minutes. Add tomatoes and cook for another 5 minutes. Stir in oregano, basil, goat cheese, and pepper and serve over fettuccine.

TUXEDO TAPENADE

SERVES 4

INGREDIENTS

1 tbsp olive oil
1 shallot, sliced
1 clove garlic, sliced
1/2 cup (125 ml) black olives, pitted
2 tbsp capers
Zest of 1/2 lemon
1/2 cup (125 ml) olive oil

PREPARATION

In a pan, sauté shallots and garlic in oil.

With a hand blender or in a food processor, combine shallots and garlic, olives, capers, and lemon zest. Add oil in a steady stream.

Serve with farfalle (bow tie pasta).

TASTY TIP

Add pork, chicken, or pan-fried fish for a quick weeknight meal.

SAFFRON SEAFOOD

SERVES 4

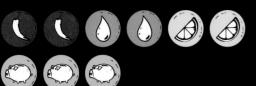

INGREDIENTS

1/2 tsp saffron
1/4 cup (60 ml) hot water
1 tbsp butter
1/2 cup (125 ml) Nordic shrimp
2 whole squids, heads and fins removed, cleaned
and cut into rounds
1/2 cup (125 ml) canned clams, drained and rinsed
1/2 cup (125 ml) dry chorizo, cut in half lengthwise
and cut into half moons
2 cloves garlic, minced
12 cherry tomatoes, halved
1/2 cup (125 ml) white wine
1/3 cup (80 ml) 35% cream
1/2 cup (125 ml) baby scallops
2 cups (500 ml) baby spinach, roughly chopped
4 drops Tabasco sauce
Juice of 1/2 lemon
Salt and freshly ground pepper

PREPARATION

Infuse saffron in hot water for 15 minutes.

In a large pot, melt butter and sauté shrimp, calamari rounds, clams, and chorizo. Add garlic, cherry tomatoes, saffron infusion, and white wine. Reduce for 2 minutes and add remaining ingredients. Season with salt and pepper and cook for another 3 to 4 minutes.

Toss with *conchiglie* (shells) and serve.

DID YOU KNOW?

If you're not sure how to prepare squid for cooking, ask your local fishmonger or a fish expert at the supermarket.

WILD MUSHROOM MADNESS

SERVES 4

INGREDIENTS

1 cup (250 ml) dried wild mushrooms
8 sundried tomatoes, thinly sliced
1 cup (250 ml) chicken stock
1 tbsp olive oil
2 green onions, thinly sliced
1/4 cup (60 ml) pecans, chopped
1 clove garlic, minced
1/2 cup (125 ml) white wine
Salt and freshly ground pepper
2 cups (500 ml) arugula

PREPARATION

Rehydrate mushrooms and tomatoes in chicken stock for 20 minutes.

Remove mushrooms and tomatoes and reserve stock. In a large pan, heat olive oil and sauté green onions, mushrooms, and tomatoes for 3 minutes. Add pecans and garlic and cook for another minute. Deglaze with white wine, add chicken stock, and season with salt and pepper. Reduce liquid by half. Gently stir in arugula and serve over *capellini*.

 **DID YOU KNOW?**

The study of fungi is called mycology.

45

SAUSAGE, TOMATO & FRESH BASIL

SERVES 4

INGREDIENTS

2 Italian sausages (any kind)
2 tbsp olive oil
2 red peppers, diced
1 onion, finely chopped
2 cloves garlic, minced
1/2 cup (125 ml) red wine
1 cup (250 ml) canned diced tomatoes
Salt and freshly ground pepper
Fresh basil, chopped

PREPARATION

Remove sausage meat from casings and form into small meatballs with your hands.

In a large pan, heat oil and cook meatballs, red peppers, and onions. Add garlic and deglaze with red wine. Add diced tomatoes, salt, and pepper. Simmer for 5 minutes. Serve over penne and garnish with fresh basil.

46

THE PURIST

SERVES 4

INGREDIENTS

1/4 cup (60 ml) high quality olive oil
4 cloves garlic, crushed
1/2 tsp crushed red pepper flakes
2 tbsp pasta cooking water
Salt and freshly ground pepper

PREPARATION

In a pan, heat olive oil and garlic cloves over low heat and cook until garlic begins to brown. Remove garlic and stir in crushed red pepper flakes. Season with salt and pepper.

Add cooked pasta of your choice and pasta water. Stir and serve.

DID YOU KNOW?

This dish is also known as *aglio e olio* (garlic and oil).

TASTY TIP

Although purists would disagree, we think it's perfectly acceptable to sprinkle some fresh Parmesan and chopped parsley onto this classically simple dish to make the flavors pop!

TUNA PUTTANESCA

SERVES 4

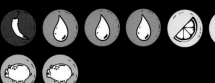

INGREDIENTS

2 tbsp olive oil
8 anchovy fillets
1 onion, finely chopped
1 tsp crushed red pepper flakes
2 cloves garlic, minced
2 tbsp capers, rinsed and chopped
1/2 cup (125 ml) black olives, rinsed, pitted and chopped
1 1/2 cups (375 ml) canned diced tomatoes
1 can (6 oz) tuna
Salt and freshly ground pepper

PREPARATION

In a pan, heat olive oil and sauté anchovies, onion, red pepper flakes, and garlic for 5 minutes. Add capers, olives, tomatoes, and tuna. Season with salt and pepper. Cover and simmer for 15 minutes. Serve over long pasta of your choice.

 **DID YOU KNOW?**

Puttanesca sauce has an interesting—and somewhat scandalous—history. The Italian word *puttanesca* translates as "in the style of the ladies of the night," and as the story goes, prostitutes would whip up this simple meal in between clients using pantry staples and the tantalizing aroma wafting into the streets would attract more customers. The ultimate comfort food!

THE RAGÙ

SERVES 4

INGREDIENTS

1/2 cup (125 ml) olive oil
1/2 lb beef stew meat, cubed
1/2 lb pork stew meat, cubed
1/2 cup thick cut bacon, cut into small cubes
2 onions, finely chopped
2 carrots, peeled and diced
2 stalks celery, diced
4 cloves garlic, chopped
1 can (6 oz) tomato paste
1 cup (250 ml) red wine
1 can (28 oz) diced tomatoes
1 bay leaf
Choice of fresh herbs (oregano, thyme, rosemary, etc.)
Salt and freshly ground pepper

PREPARATION

In a Dutch oven or heavy-bottomed oven-safe pot, heat oil and sear beef and pork until golden brown. Remove and set aside. In the same pot, sauté bacon, onions, carrots, celery, and garlic, about 5 minutes. Add tomato paste and cook for another 2 minutes. Transfer meat back to pot and add red wine, tomatoes, bay leaf, and herbs of your choice. Season with salt and pepper.

Cover and cook in a 300°F (150°C) oven for 2 to 3 hours. Serve over pasta of your choice.

SPAGHETTI SQUASH

SERVES 4

INGREDIENTS

3 tbsp olive oil
1/2 spaghetti squash, seeds removed
Salt and freshly ground pepper
1 onion, finely chopped
6 slices bacon, cut into small strips
1 1/2 cups (375 ml) pomodoro sauce (see recipe on page 032)
1/2 cup (125 ml) fresh basil, thinly sliced
1/3 cup (80 ml) fresh Parmesan cheese, grated

PREPARATION

Brush inside of squash with 2 tbsp olive oil. Season with salt and pepper and place on a baking sheet. Bake in a 350°F (175°C) oven for 1 hour or until flesh can be easily removed with a spoon.

Remove flesh and set aside.

In a large pan, sauté onions and bacon in remaining 1 tbsp olive oil. Add spaghetti squash, stir, and cook for 2 minutes. Add pomodoro sauce and simmer for 4 minutes. Add basil and Parmesan cheese and serve over spaghetti.

Express version: Cut squash into 4 pieces and discard seeds. Place squash pieces in a casserole dish with a bit of water. Cover and cook in the microwave, about 12 minutes.

TASTY TIP

Spaghetti squash is a great substitute for pasta if you're trying to cut down on carbohydrates. Just double the squash in this recipe and omit the pasta for a healthy, delicious meal.

CARAMELIZED OINION SAUCE

SERVES 4

INGREDIENTS

1 tbsp butter
1 sprig fresh rosemary
4 onions, thinly sliced
1 tbsp sugar
1/2 cup (125 ml) water
Pomodoro sauce (see recipe on page 032)
Salt and freshly ground pepper

PREPARATION

In a large pot, heat all ingredients except pomodoro sauce. Cook for 20 minutes over medium heat, stirring occasionally, until onions become caramelized. Add water, stir, and cook until liquid has fully evaporated.

Add pomodoro sauce and season with salt and pepper. Simmer for 5 minutes and serve over pasta of your choice.

 DID YOU KNOW?

When you caramelize onions, you're browning the natural sugars they contain, resulting in a darker color and nutty caramel flavor.

 TASTY TIP

If your kids just won't eat onions, get a little sneaky and purée the caramelized onions and pomodoro into a smooth sauce. They'll love the sweet flavor and—you never know—they might just ask for seconds!

TOMATO CONFIT

SERVES 4

INGREDIENTS

12 Italian tomatoes, halved, stems removed
4 cloves garlic, thinly sliced
4 sprigs fresh thyme
4 sprigs fresh rosemary
1 tsp salt
1 tsp freshly ground pepper
1 tbsp sugar
1/2 cup (125 ml) olive oil

PREPARATION

Arrange tomatoes on a baking sheet, cut sides up, and place a slice of garlic on each. Scatter thyme and rosemary evenly over halves and sprinkle with salt, pepper, and sugar. Drizzle generously with olive oil and cook in a 275°F (135°C) oven for 3 hours.

Serve tomatoes whole, roughly chopped, or puréed over the pasta of your choice.

 TASTY TIP

Use the leftover oil from the baking sheet to coat pasta or reserve it and use it to add flavor to another recipe!

THAI DELIGHT

SERVES 4

INGREDIENTS

1 tbsp canola oil
1 tbsp sesame oil
1/2 leek, brunoised
2 cloves garlic, minced
2 tbsp ginger, minced
1/4 cup (60 ml) soy sauce
1/4 cup (60 ml) oyster sauce
1 tbsp brown sugar
1/4 cup (60 ml) canola oil
2 tbsp black and white sesame seeds, toasted
1/4 cup (60 ml) chives, chopped

PREPARATION

In a pot, heat 1 tbsp canola oil and sesame oil. Sauté leek, garlic, and half of the ginger. Add soy sauce, oyster sauce, brown sugar, and remaining canola oil and simmer for 10 minutes. Remove from heat and add remaining ginger, sesame seeds, and chives. Serve over rice vermicelli and sautéed vegetables of your choice.

DID YOU KNOW?

In India, sesame seeds are an ancient symbol of immortality.

PERFECT PORCINI

SERVES 4

INGREDIENTS

3/4 cup (180 ml) dried porcini mushrooms
OR 2 cups (500 ml) fresh porcini mushrooms, thinly sliced
2 tbsp olive oil
1 onion, finely chopped
1/3 cup (80 ml) white wine
1/4 cup (60 ml) fresh parsley, chopped
Salt and freshly ground pepper
Parmesan cheese for garnish

PREPARATION

Rehydrate mushrooms by immersing them in water for 15 minutes. Drain.

Cook mushrooms in a hot unoiled pan until excess water has evaporated. Add olive oil and onion and sauté for a few minutes. Add white wine, 2 tbsp pasta water, parsley, salt, and pepper. Serve over penne and garnish with Parmesan cheese shavings.

 **DID YOU KNOW?**

Porcini actually means "piglets" in Italian, and were likely given this name because of their plump form when found on forest floors.

THE ALFREDO

SERVES 4

INGREDIENTS

3/4 cup (180 ml) 35% cream
Salt
Freshly ground black pepper
3/4 cup (180 ml) fresh Parmesan cheese, grated

PREPARATION

Cook cream, salt and pepper in a large pan for 2 minutes until cream is reduced. Add fettucine and Parmesan cheese. Toss well and serve.

Alfredo is the perfect accompaniment to any dish. Just add your favorite ingredients, like chicken or shrimp and your choice of vegetables, to turn it into a memorable main course!

TASTY TIP

Try a nutty Swiss Gruyère instead of Parmesan.

56

THE PIEDMONTESE

SERVES 4

INGREDIENTS

2 tbsp butter
1 shallot, minced
2 cups (500 ml) wild mushrooms of your choice
(oyster mushrooms, chanterelles, blue foot mushrooms, etc.)
1 cup (250 ml) store-bought demi-glace
1/2 tsp nutmeg
1/4 cup (60 ml) truffle paste (optional)
1/4 cup (60 ml) fresh Parmesan cheese, grated
Salt and freshly ground pepper

PREPARATION

In a pan, sauté shallots and mushrooms in butter.

Add demi-glace, nutmeg, and truffle paste. Reduce until sauce is velvety and coats the back of a spoon. Season with salt and pepper.

Stir in Parmesan cheese and serve over long egg noodles.

 **DID YOU KNOW?**

The rare white truffle, often called "the diamond of the kitchen," comes from the Piedmont region of northern Italy and is the most valuable food in the world. In 2005, a truffle weighing 3.3 pounds was sold for US$330,000! It is also considered an aphrodisiac.

57

THE BÉCHAMEL

SERVES 4

 **DID YOU KNOW?**

Béchamel is a versatile white sauce that many chefs consider to be the king of all sauces! It is the foundation for gravies, creamy casseroles, and soufflés, and, obviously, any classic lasagna recipe.

 TASTY TIP

Experiment with different flavors by adding puréed squash or eggplant, pesto, or chopped spinach to your béchamel sauce. The sky's the limit!

INGREDIENTS

3 tbsp butter
1 onion, finely chopped
3 tbsp flour
2 cups (500 ml) milk
1/2 tsp nutmeg, grated
Salt and freshly ground pepper

PREPARATION

In a pot, melt butter and sauté onion. Add flour and cook for 30 seconds, whisking constantly to prevent lumps from forming. Whisk in 1/4 cup milk. Slowly pour in remaining milk, whisking constantly. Add nutmeg and season with salt and pepper. Simmer, whisking constantly, until sauce becomes thick. Remove from heat.

Use this creamy béchamel in your favorite lasagna recipe.

166 | THE WORLD'S 60 BEST PASTA SAUCES

ITALIAN "CINQUE PI" SAUCE

SERVES 4

INGREDIENTS

1 1/2 cups (375 ml) pomodoro sauce (see recipe on page 032)
1/4 cup (60 ml) fresh Parmesan cheese
1/4 cup (60 ml) 35% cream
2 tbsp fresh parsley, chopped
Freshly ground pepper

PREPARATION

In a pot, heat pomodoro sauce and add Parmesan cheese, cream, parsley, and pepper.

Let simmer for a few minutes to allow flavors to blend. Serve over medaglioni or stuffed pasta of your choice.

DID YOU KNOW?

Cinque Pi sauce is a tomato-based Italian sauce. Its name comes from the first letter of its five ingredients: *panna* (cream), *pomodoro* (tomato), *parmigiano* (Parmesan), *prezzemolo* (parsley) and *pepe* (pepper).

THE BOLOGNESE

SERVES 4

INGREDIENTS

1 onion, quartered
2 cloves garlic
2 carrots, roughly chopped
2 celery stalks, roughly chopped
10 mushrooms
1 tsp olive oil
1 can (6 oz) tomato paste
1 lb ground beef
1 cup (250 ml) beef stock
1 can (14 oz) tomato juice
1 can (28 oz) crushed tomatoes
Salt and freshly ground pepper
1 tbsp sugar
1 tsp crushed red pepper flakes
2 bay leaves
1 tbsp Italian seasoning

PREPARATION

In a food processor, pulse onion, garlic, carrots, celery, and mushrooms until all ingredients are coarsely chopped.

In a Dutch oven or heavy-bottomed pot, heat oil and sauté chopped vegetables. Add tomato paste and ground beef and cook for 10 more minutes. Add remaining ingredients. Reduce heat and simmer for 2 hours, stirring frequently. Serve over spaghetti.

 **TASTY TIP**

Make traditional bolognese with a twist by using game or adding wild mushrooms!

THE GRATIN

SERVES 4

INGREDIENTS

2 cups (500 ml) mozzarella cheese, grated

1 pasta recipe of your choice

PREPARATION

Spread mozzarella cheese evenly over the pasta and sauce of your choice. Broil until cheese becomes golden brown.

We know, gratin isn't a *sauce*.
But there's no denying it's one of the best ways to reinvent the old, dried-out pasta left over in the refrigerator!

Instead of taking the time to make a whole new batch of sauce or resorting to a bland store-bought version, just pop a gratin into the oven for a quick, easy, deliciously comforting meal.

TASTY TIP

Mozzarella is the *best* cheese for gratins because it becomes so wonderfully golden under the broiler, but it's not the only cheese you can use! Experiment with your favorite cheeses and discover new flavor combinations.

INGREDIENTS INDEX

CONVERSION CHART

1 dl	10 cl	100 ml
1 tablespoon		15 ml
1 teaspoon		5 ml
1 oz.		30 ml
1 cup		250 ml
4 cups		1 l
1/2 cup		125 ml
1/4 cup		60 ml
1/3 cup		80 ml
1 lb		450 g
2 lbs		900 g
2.2 lbs		1 kg
400°F	200°C	T/7
350°F	175°C	T/6
300°F	150°C	T/5

Volume Conversion
* Approximate values

---

1 cup (250 ml) crumbled cheese	150 g
1 cup (250 ml) all-purpose flour	115 g
1 cup (250 ml) white sugar	200 g
1 cup (250 ml) brown sugar	220 g
1 cup (250 ml) butter	230 g
1 cup (250 ml) oil	215 g
1 cup (250 ml) canned tomatoes	250 g

NOTES

IN THE SAME COLLECTION

THE WORLD'S **60** BEST

SALADS

PERIOD.

THE WORLD'S **60** BEST

BURGERS

PERIOD.